Daily

Affirmations

for

Health

Overcome Stress & Anxiety, Nurture Mental & Physical Health, , and Cultivate Effective Habits for Healing and Recovery

OTHER BOOKS BY AUTHOR

1. 9 Secrets of subconscious mind
2. Unlock your subconscious mind
3. Rewire your beliefs
4. Secrets of happy life
5. Secrets of happy family
6. Everyday happiness
7. Instant happiness quotes
8. Workbook – Practice to be happy
9. Positive Affirmations for success
10. MONEY Affirmations that work

Download E-book for FREE

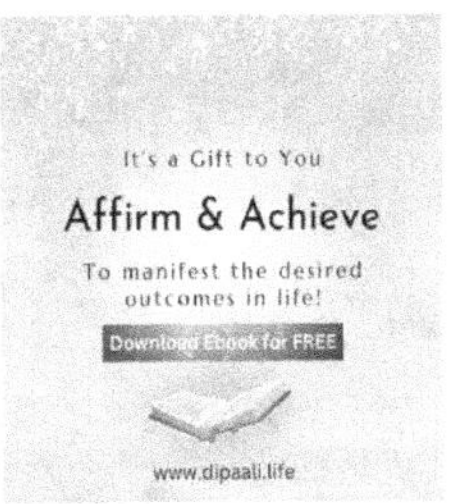

Our thoughts and words shape our reality, so it's essential to monitor and transform any negative thoughts before expressing them. Spoken words possess the power to change our destiny. By downloading a free e-book, you can access a list of empowering affirmations designed to counteract negative self-talk. Practicing these affirmations daily, along with utilizing nine manifestation secrets, can help you achieve desired outcomes in all areas of your life.

Click here to download eBook for free

COPYRIGHT@2024 BY DIPAALI PATEL

INTRODUCTION

In today's fast-paced world, achieving and maintaining optimal health requires more than just physical care; it necessitates a balanced approach that nurtures both body and mind. "Health Affirmations for Body and Mind" is crafted to guide you on this transformative journey, offering a holistic blend of practices designed to enhance your overall well-being. This book provides a powerful toolkit of affirmations, each aimed at fostering a harmonious connection between mental and physical health.

Chapter 1, Foundation of Health: Mind-Body Connection

Our journey begins with understanding the profound relationship between mind and body. This chapter highlights the importance of a balanced lifestyle where mental and physical health are interconnected. By embracing these affirmations, you will learn to harmonize your thoughts and emotions with physical practices, leading to a more integrated and resilient you. The benefits include improved overall health and a deeper sense of inner peace.

Chapter 2, Physical Wellness

Physical wellness is fundamental to living a vibrant life. This chapter offers affirmations that encourage regular exercise, nutritious eating, and overall bodily care. By incorporating these practices, you will promote your physical health, boost your energy levels, and enhance your quality of life. These affirmations help you establish and maintain habits that support long-term physical well-being.

Chapter 3, Mental and Emotional Well-Being

Mental and emotional stability are essential for navigating life's ups and downs. This chapter focuses on affirmations that support mental health, emotional balance, and resilience against stress and anxiety. By fostering a positive mindset, these affirmations empower you to handle life's challenges with grace and confidence, leading to greater emotional stability and well-being.

Chapter 4, Healing and Recovery

For those on the path to recovery from illness or injury, this chapter provides affirmations that promote healing and strength. These affirmations encourage a mindset of recovery and resilience, helping you to remain focused on your healing journey and regain your vitality. They are designed to support and accelerate the healing process, both physically and emotionally.

Chapter 5, Healthy Habits and Routines

Consistency in daily habits is key to sustained health. This chapter offers affirmations that encourage the development and maintenance of healthy routines. By integrating these affirmations into your daily life, you will cultivate habits that support long-term wellness and foster a balanced lifestyle. The result is a more organized, healthy, and fulfilling life.

Chapter 6, Stress Management and Relaxation

Managing stress effectively is crucial for maintaining overall health. This chapter provides affirmations focused on stress relief, relaxation techniques, and the importance of rest. By practicing these affirmations, you will learn to reduce stress, enhance relaxation, and improve your overall quality of life, leading to greater mental clarity and tranquility.

Chapter 7, Self-Love and Body Positivity

Embracing self-love and body positivity is essential for a healthy self-image. This chapter offers affirmations that promote self-acceptance, self-love, and a positive body image. By fostering these positive attitudes, you will build a more compassionate and confident relationship with yourself, leading to improved self-esteem and overall happiness.

Chapter 8, Energy and Vitality

Energizing your life is crucial for achieving peak performance and enthusiasm. This chapter provides affirmations designed to boost your energy levels and vitality. By incorporating these affirmations, you will enhance your enthusiasm for life, increase your motivation, and enjoy a more vibrant and active lifestyle.

Chapter 9, Holistic Health and Well-Being

Our final chapter encompasses a holistic approach to health, integrating mind, body, and spirit. These affirmations aim to foster a comprehensive sense of well-being by aligning all aspects of your life. By embracing this holistic perspective, you will achieve a balanced and harmonious state of health, enhancing your overall well-being and fulfillment.

"Health Affirmations for Body and Mind" is more than just a collection of positive statements; it's a roadmap to a healthier, more balanced life. Each chapter is designed to address key aspects of your well-being, guiding you towards a state of complete health and vitality.

TABLE OF CONTENT

CHAPTER 1, FOUNDATION OF HEALTH: MIND-BODY CONNECTION

1. I am in perfect harmony with my mind and body.
2. My body is a vessel of strength and wellness.
3. I listen to my body's signals and respond with love and care.
4. My mind is calm, clear, and focused.
5. I nourish my body with healthy, nutritious foods.
6. I am grateful for my healthy body and mind.
7. I am at peace with myself and my surroundings.
8. My mind and body work together to achieve optimal health.
9. I embrace a lifestyle that promotes balance and well-being.
10. My thoughts are positive and uplifting.

11. I am deserving of good health and happiness.
12. I honor and respect my body's needs.
13. My mind is a powerful tool for healing and growth.
14. I am in tune with my body's wisdom.
15. I create a healthy and happy life for myself.
16. I release any stress and tension from my mind and body.
17. My body is resilient and capable of healing.
18. I prioritize self-care and make time for relaxation.
19. I am connected to the present moment and find joy in it.
20. My mind is a source of positivity and inspiration.
21. I trust my body's ability to heal and thrive.
22. I am grateful for the strength and vitality of my body.

23. My thoughts and actions align with my health goals.
24. I am committed to maintaining a healthy mind and body.
25. I practice mindfulness and stay present in every moment.
26. My body is a reflection of my inner well-being.
27. I am in control of my thoughts and emotions.
28. I am worthy of love, health, and happiness.
29. I choose to think thoughts that support my health and well-being.
30. I am a magnet for positive energy and good health.
31. My body responds positively to healthy habits.
32. I embrace change and growth with an open mind.
33. I am grateful for the abundance of health in my life.

34. My mind is my greatest ally in achieving my health goals.
35. I am kind and gentle with myself.
36. I let go of any negative thoughts and replace them with positivity.
37. I am in tune with my body's natural rhythms.
38. I prioritize my mental and physical health every day.
39. I am surrounded by healing energy.
40. I am capable of achieving a balanced and healthy life.
41. My mind and body are connected and work in harmony.
42. I am at peace with who I am.
43. I choose to focus on the positive aspects of my health.
44. I am strong, healthy, and full of energy.
45. I take deep breaths and feel calm and centered.
46. I am grateful for my body and all it does for me.

47. My mind is clear and focused on my well-being.
48. I am committed to living a healthy and fulfilling life.
49. I trust the journey of my life and my health.
50. I am surrounded by positive, healing energy.
51. I am in control of my health and well-being.
52. My body is strong, capable, and resilient.
53. I am grateful for the health and vitality of my body.
54. I honor my body's needs and listen to its signals.
55. My mind is calm, clear, and focused on the present moment.
56. I am deserving of good health and happiness.
57. I am at peace with my body and my mind.
58. I am in tune with my body's wisdom and intuition.

59. I am committed to maintaining a healthy lifestyle.
60. My thoughts are positive and supportive of my health.
61. I am grateful for the abundance of health in my life.
62. My mind is a powerful tool for healing and growth.
63. I am surrounded by positive energy and good health.
64. I am worthy of love, health, and happiness.
65. I choose to think thoughts that support my health and well-being.
66. I am a magnet for positive energy and good health.
67. My body responds positively to healthy habits.
68. I embrace change and growth with an open mind.
69. I am grateful for the strength and vitality of my body.

70. My thoughts and actions align with my health goals.

71. I am committed to maintaining a healthy mind and body.

72. I practice mindfulness and stay present in every moment.

73. My body is a reflection of my inner well-being.

74. I am in control of my thoughts and emotions.

75. I am kind and gentle with myself.

76. I let go of any negative thoughts and replace them with positivity.

77. I am in tune with my body's natural rhythms.

78. I prioritize my mental and physical health every day.

79. I am surrounded by healing energy.

80. I am capable of achieving a balanced and healthy life.

81. My mind and body are connected and work in harmony.

82. I am at peace with who I am.

83. I choose to focus on the positive aspects of my health.

84. I am strong, healthy, and full of energy.

85. I take deep breaths and feel calm and centered.

86. I am grateful for my body and all it does for me.

87. My mind is clear and focused on my well-being.

88. I am committed to living a healthy and fulfilling life.

89. I trust the journey of my life and my health.

90. I am surrounded by positive, healing energy.

91. I am in control of my health and well-being.

92. My body is strong, capable, and resilient.

93. I am grateful for the health and vitality of my body.

94. I honor my body's needs and listen to its signals.
95. My mind is calm, clear, and focused on the present moment.
96. I am deserving of good health and happiness.
97. I am at peace with my body and my mind.
98. I am in tune with my body's wisdom and intuition.
99. I am committed to maintaining a healthy lifestyle.
100. My thoughts are positive and supportive of my health.

CHAPTER 2, PHYSICAL WELLNESS

1. I am strong and capable.
2. My body is a beautiful gift, and I cherish it.
3. I nourish my body with healthy foods.
4. Exercise is a celebration of what my body can do.
5. I am grateful for my healthy body.
6. My body deserves love and respect.
7. I listen to my body's needs.
8. I am committed to my physical well-being.
9. I choose to eat foods that nourish my body.
10. I enjoy moving my body in ways that feel good.
11. My health is a priority.
12. I am patient with my body's progress.
13. Every day, I am becoming stronger.
14. I love and appreciate my body.
15. Healthy habits are a part of my daily life.
16. I treat my body with kindness and respect.
17. I am in charge of my health and happiness.

18. My body is resilient and capable of healing.
19. I love feeling strong and fit.
20. I enjoy the process of becoming healthier.
21. I am proud of my physical achievements.
22. I am in tune with my body's needs.
23. I make time for self-care.
24. I enjoy the vitality that comes from regular exercise.
25. I am grateful for the ability to move my body.
26. I am becoming more energetic every day.
27. I choose to be active and fit.
28. I honor my body by treating it well.
29. I am worthy of good health.
30. I have the power to create change in my body.
31. Every day, I make choices that benefit my health.
32. I am dedicated to living a healthy lifestyle.
33. I love the feeling of being active and alive.

34. My body is a reflection of my inner strength.
35. I choose foods that fuel my body.
36. I am grateful for my body's strength and endurance.
37. I am committed to exercising regularly.
38. I enjoy discovering new ways to stay fit.
39. My body is my home, and I care for it deeply.
40. I feel vibrant and full of energy.
41. I am constantly improving my health.
42. I embrace a lifestyle of wellness.
43. I am grateful for my body's ability to move.
44. I am strong, healthy, and vibrant.
45. I take care of my body, mind, and spirit.
46. I am committed to eating nourishing foods.
47. I find joy in taking care of my physical health.
48. My body responds positively to healthy habits.
49. I am in love with my body and all it can do.

50. I celebrate the progress I make in my physical health.
51. I feel great after exercising.
52. I am proud of my commitment to fitness.
53. I am grateful for the strength and flexibility of my body.
54. I treat my body with the care it deserves.
55. I am constantly learning about ways to improve my health.
56. I enjoy eating foods that make me feel good.
57. I choose to prioritize my physical well-being.
58. I am grateful for my body's ability to heal and recover.
59. I enjoy the journey of becoming healthier.
60. I am proud of the healthy choices I make.
61. I am dedicated to maintaining my physical health.
62. I love the way exercise makes me feel.
63. I am grateful for my body's ability to move and be active.

64. I am committed to living a healthy and active life.
65. I respect my body and listen to its needs.
66. I enjoy the feeling of being fit and healthy.
67. I am proud of my efforts to take care of my body.
68. I am grateful for my body's strength and resilience.
69. I love the feeling of being strong and capable.
70. I am committed to making healthy choices every day.
71. I am grateful for the energy and vitality I feel.
72. I enjoy the process of improving my physical health.
73. I am proud of my dedication to fitness.
74. I am grateful for my body's ability to move and be active.
75. I am committed to living a healthy and active life.
76. I respect my body and listen to its needs.

77. I enjoy the feeling of being fit and healthy.

78. I am proud of my efforts to take care of my body.

79. I am grateful for my body's strength and resilience.

80. I love the feeling of being strong and capable.

81. I am committed to making healthy choices every day.

82. I am grateful for the energy and vitality I feel.

83. I enjoy the process of improving my physical health.

84. I am proud of my dedication to fitness.

85. I am grateful for my body's ability to move and be active.

86. I am committed to living a healthy and active life.

87. I respect my body and listen to its needs.

88. I enjoy the feeling of being fit and healthy.

89. I am proud of my efforts to take care of my body.

90. I am grateful for my body's strength and resilience.
91. I love the feeling of being strong and capable.
92. I am committed to making healthy choices every day.
93. I am grateful for the energy and vitality I feel.
94. I enjoy the process of improving my physical health.
95. I am proud of my dedication to fitness.
96. I am grateful for my body's ability to move and be active.
97. I am committed to living a healthy and active life.
98. I respect my body and listen to its needs.
99. I enjoy the feeling of being fit and healthy.
100. I am proud of my efforts to take care of my body.

CHAPTER 3: MENTAL AND EMOTIONAL WELL-BEING

1. I am in control of my thoughts and emotions.
2. I am worthy of love and happiness.
3. I choose to focus on the positive in every situation.
4. I am resilient and can handle any challenges that come my way.
5. My mind is calm and centered.
6. I embrace my feelings and honor my emotions.
7. I am at peace with my past and excited for my future.
8. I release all negativity and welcome positivity into my life.
9. I am strong, capable, and confident.
10. My mind is clear and focused.
11. I am deserving of emotional stability and balance.

12. I handle stress with grace and ease.

13. I am proud of who I am becoming.

14. My emotional well-being is a priority.

15. I am surrounded by supportive and loving people.

16. I choose to let go of worry and embrace peace.

17. I trust myself and my decisions.

18. I am calm in the face of adversity.

19. I accept myself unconditionally.

20. I am grateful for the present moment.

21. I am in charge of my own happiness.

22. I am a work in progress, and that's okay.

23. I allow myself to feel and express my emotions.

24. I am gentle with myself and others.

25. I am confident in my ability to overcome challenges.

26. My mind is a source of creativity and positivity.

27. I am worthy of all the good things life has to offer.

28. I am capable of achieving my goals and dreams.
29. I choose to see the good in every situation.
30. I am at peace with who I am.
31. I embrace change and growth.
32. I am strong, resilient, and capable of handling stress.
33. I release the need to control everything.
34. I trust the process of life.
35. I am grateful for the lessons learned through challenges.
36. I am calm and centered even in difficult situations.
37. I am worthy of love, respect, and kindness.
38. I embrace my unique qualities and strengths.
39. I am in control of my reactions to stress.
40. I choose to think positively about myself and my life.
41. I am capable of handling any emotions that arise.

42. I am patient with myself as I grow and evolve.
43. I am open to new experiences and opportunities.
44. I am grateful for my mental and emotional strength.
45. I am at peace with my past and excited about my future.
46. I am confident in my ability to manage stress effectively.
47. I am deserving of a fulfilling and joyful life.
48. I am surrounded by positivity and love.
49. I am in tune with my emotions and needs.
50. I am capable of creating a peaceful and balanced life.
51. I am grateful for the support and love in my life.
52. I am open to receiving all the good things life has to offer.
53. I am resilient and bounce back from challenges stronger.

54. I am worthy of experiencing joy and happiness.

55. I am in control of my mental and emotional state.

56. I am capable of achieving emotional balance and stability.

57. I choose to release fear and embrace courage.

58. I am kind and compassionate towards myself.

59. I am grateful for the strength that comes from overcoming obstacles.

60. I am calm and centered, even in stressful situations.

61. I am worthy of peace and contentment.

62. I am in tune with my inner self and emotions.

63. I am capable of handling stress and anxiety with ease.

64. I am confident in my ability to create positive change in my life.

65. I am open to receiving love and support from others.
66. I am grateful for the growth and learning that comes from challenges.
67. I am deserving of mental and emotional peace.
68. I am resilient and can adapt to any situation.
69. I am at peace with who I am and where I am in life.
70. I am open to new perspectives and ideas.
71. I am capable of managing my emotions effectively.
72. I am surrounded by positivity and support.
73. I am grateful for my ability to overcome obstacles.
74. I am confident in my ability to maintain emotional balance.
75. I am deserving of happiness and fulfillment.
76. I am strong, capable, and worthy of success.

77. I am at peace with my past and excited for my future.
78. I am open to the flow of positive energy in my life.
79. I am confident in my ability to handle stress and challenges.
80. I am deserving of love, respect, and kindness from others and myself.
81. I am grateful for the strength and resilience I possess.
82. I am calm, centered, and focused on my well-being.
83. I am in control of my thoughts and choose positivity.
84. I am worthy of experiencing joy and happiness in my life.
85. I am resilient and capable of overcoming any obstacle.
86. I am open to receiving all the love and support I need.
87. I am grateful for the positive changes happening in my life.

88. I am confident in my ability to create a peaceful and balanced life.
89. I am deserving of mental and emotional well-being.
90. I am surrounded by supportive and loving people.
91. I am calm and composed in the face of challenges.
92. I am grateful for the strength and resilience within me.
93. I am capable of achieving emotional stability and balance.
94. I am open to new experiences and opportunities for growth.
95. I am worthy of all the good things that life has to offer.
96. I am confident in my ability to handle stress and anxiety.
97. I am grateful for my mental and emotional strength.
98. I am deserving of love, respect, and happiness.

99. I am calm and centered, even in difficult times.

100. I am open to embracing positivity and letting go of negativity.

CHAPTER 4: HEALING AND RECOVERY

1. I am healing every day.
2. My body is strong and resilient.
3. I trust my body to heal itself.
4. I am surrounded by love and support.
5. Every cell in my body vibrates with health.
6. I am patient with my healing journey.
7. My mind and body are in perfect harmony.
8. I am grateful for my body's ability to heal.
9. I embrace the process of healing.
10. I am getting stronger every day.
11. My spirit is unbreakable.
12. I nourish my body with healthy choices.
13. I am worthy of good health.
14. I choose to be positive in my healing journey.
15. My body knows how to heal itself.
16. I am resilient and persistent.
17. I am at peace with my healing process.
18. I am releasing all tension from my body.

19. My energy is focused on healing.

20. I am becoming healthier every day.

21. I am grateful for my body's strength.

22. I am in tune with my body's needs.

23. I am open to receiving healing energy.

24. I am worthy of a full recovery.

25. My body is a miraculous vessel.

26. I trust the process of healing.

27. I am surrounded by positive energy.

28. I am releasing all negative thoughts.

29. I am filled with healing light.

30. I am grateful for the support I receive.

31. I am becoming my healthiest self.

32. I am patient with my progress.

33. I am grateful for my body's capabilities.

34. I am healing from within.

35. I am worthy of a pain-free life.

36. I am sending love to every part of my body.

37. I am becoming stronger every day.

38. I am grateful for my body's resilience.

39. I am surrounded by healing energy.

40. I am worthy of health and happiness.

41. I am at peace with my recovery process.

42. I am releasing all fear and doubt.

43. I am embracing my body's natural healing abilities.

44. I am grateful for each step in my recovery.

45. I am connected to the healing power of the universe.

46. I am worthy of a healthy body and mind.

47. I am embracing positive change.

48. I am healing with every breath I take.

49. I am open to the healing power of love.

50. I am grateful for my body's ability to heal.

51. I am surrounded by healing and love.

52. I am worthy of complete recovery.

53. I am embracing my body's natural strength.

54. I am releasing all pain and discomfort.

55. I am patient and gentle with myself.

56. I am grateful for the progress I've made.

57. I am healing at my own pace.

58. I am worthy of a vibrant, healthy life.

59. I am surrounded by positive, healing energy.
60. I am grateful for my body's resilience.
61. I am connecting with my inner strength.
62. I am healing from the inside out.
63. I am worthy of a life free from pain.
64. I am embracing my healing journey.
65. I am filled with gratitude for my body's healing.
66. I am releasing all negativity.
67. I am open to the healing power of the universe.
68. I am grateful for the love and support I receive.
69. I am becoming healthier every day.
70. I am patient with my healing process.
71. I am surrounded by positive energy.
72. I am worthy of a full and complete recovery.
73. I am grateful for my body's strength.
74. I am healing in mind, body, and spirit.
75. I am releasing all tension and stress.

76. I am open to receiving healing energy.

77. I am worthy of a healthy, balanced life.

78. I am grateful for my body's ability to heal.

79. I am surrounded by healing love and light.

80. I am embracing positive thoughts and feelings.

81. I am patient with my body's healing process.

82. I am worthy of a life full of health and happiness.

83. I am grateful for the progress I've made.

84. I am healing with each passing moment.

85. I am releasing all fear and embracing healing.

86. I am open to the healing power of love and light.

87. I am grateful for my body's resilience.

88. I am surrounded by positive, healing energy.

89. I am embracing my body's natural healing abilities.

90. I am worthy of complete wellness.

91. I am patient and kind to myself during my recovery.
92. I am grateful for the support and love I receive.
93. I am healing in every way.
94. I am releasing all pain and embracing health.
95. I am open to the healing energy of the universe.
96. I am worthy of a pain-free, healthy life.
97. I am grateful for my body's strength and resilience.
98. I am surrounded by love and healing light.
99. I am becoming stronger and healthier every day.
100. I am at peace with my healing journey.

CHAPTER 5: HEALTHY HABITS AND ROUTINES

1. I am committed to living a healthy and balanced life.
2. Every day, I am becoming healthier and stronger.
3. My body deserves love and care, and I provide it with nutritious foods.
4. I enjoy exercising and keeping my body fit.
5. I am grateful for my strong and healthy body.
6. I make time for self-care because I am worth it.
7. I choose to nourish my mind and body with positive thoughts and actions.
8. I listen to my body's needs and respond with love and kindness.

9. I prioritize sleep to rejuvenate my mind and body.

10. I am disciplined and consistent in my healthy habits.

11. I am in control of my health and well-being.

12. I love and respect my body, and I treat it with care.

13. I find joy in taking care of myself.

14. I release any habits that do not serve my highest good.

15. My healthy habits bring me peace and happiness.

16. I am patient with myself as I develop new habits.

17. I am worthy of feeling healthy and vibrant.

18. I am empowered to make healthy choices every day.

19. I choose to be active and engage in activities that I enjoy.

20. My daily routines contribute to my overall well-being.

21. I am mindful of my actions and their impact on my health.

22. I am capable of achieving my health goals.

23. I am dedicated to my health and wellness journey.

24. I am surrounded by positive influences that support my healthy lifestyle.

25. I embrace a lifestyle of balance and moderation.

26. I am grateful for the energy that healthy living gives me.

27. I make time for relaxation and stress relief.

28. I am committed to drinking enough water every day.

29. I enjoy preparing and eating healthy meals.

30. I am mindful of my eating habits and choose foods that nourish me.

31. I am proud of the progress I make toward a healthier life.

32. I trust my intuition to guide me toward healthy choices.

33. I am resilient and can overcome any challenge to my health.
34. I release any guilt or shame associated with past habits.
35. I am constantly learning and growing in my wellness journey.
36. I am deserving of good health and happiness.
37. I prioritize my mental health as much as my physical health.
38. I am confident in my ability to maintain healthy routines.
39. I am grateful for the opportunity to improve my health every day.
40. I choose to focus on the positive aspects of my health.
41. I am surrounded by a supportive community that encourages my healthy habits.
42. I am patient and gentle with myself on my health journey.

43. I am committed to practicing mindfulness and meditation.
44. I am grateful for the strength and vitality of my body.
45. I am consistent in my efforts to maintain a healthy lifestyle.
46. I am motivated to make choices that benefit my well-being.
47. I am proud of the healthy habits I am developing.
48. I am in tune with my body's needs and respond accordingly.
49. I am excited about the positive changes I am making in my life.
50. I am committed to reducing stress and promoting relaxation.
51. I am grateful for the abundance of healthy food options available to me.
52. I am dedicated to moving my body every day.
53. I am worthy of a life filled with health and wellness.

54. I am capable of achieving and maintaining my ideal weight.

55. I am grateful for the progress I have made on my health journey.

56. I am surrounded by positive energy that supports my healthy habits.

57. I am committed to making time for myself every day.

58. I am grateful for the strength and flexibility of my body.

59. I am confident in my ability to make healthy choices.

60. I am mindful of the impact of my habits on my overall well-being.

61. I am grateful for the opportunity to nurture my body and mind.

62. I am excited about the healthy future I am creating for myself.

63. I am committed to practicing gratitude and positivity every day.

64. I am worthy of taking time to care for myself.

65. I am grateful for the support and encouragement of others on my wellness journey.

66. I am proud of my commitment to a healthy lifestyle.

67. I am in control of my health and make choices that benefit me.

68. I am grateful for the ability to move my body and stay active.

69. I am committed to creating and maintaining a healthy environment.

70. I am mindful of the importance of balance in my life.

71. I am grateful for the opportunity to learn and grow in my health journey.

72. I am dedicated to practicing self-love and self-care.

73. I am confident in my ability to overcome any health challenges.

74. I am committed to making healthy habits a priority in my life.

75. I am grateful for the positive changes I am making in my health.
76. I am surrounded by positive influences that support my wellness.
77. I am committed to reducing stress and promoting relaxation.
78. I am grateful for the strength and vitality of my body.
79. I am consistent in my efforts to maintain a healthy lifestyle.
80. I am motivated to make choices that benefit my well-being.
81. I am proud of the healthy habits I am developing.
82. I am in tune with my body's needs and respond accordingly.
83. I am excited about the positive changes I am making in my life.
84. I am committed to reducing stress and promoting relaxation.
85. I am grateful for the abundance of healthy food options available to me.

86. I am dedicated to moving my body every day.
87. I am worthy of a life filled with health and wellness.
88. I am capable of achieving and maintaining my ideal weight.
89. I am grateful for the progress I have made on my health journey.
90. I am surrounded by positive energy that supports my healthy habits.
91. I am committed to making time for myself every day.
92. I am grateful for the strength and flexibility of my body.
93. I am confident in my ability to make healthy choices.
94. I am mindful of the impact of my habits on my overall well-being.
95. I am grateful for the opportunity to nurture my body and mind.
96. I am excited about the healthy future I am creating for myself.

97. I am committed to practicing gratitude and positivity every day.

98. I am worthy of taking time to care for myself.

99. I am grateful for the support and encouragement of others on my wellness journey.

100.	I am proud of my commitment to a healthy lifestyle.

CHAPTER 6: STRESS MANAGEMENT AND RELAXATION

1. I release all tension from my body and mind.
2. I am calm, peaceful, and relaxed.
3. I breathe in relaxation and breathe out tension.
4. I am in control of my stress levels.
5. My mind is calm and my body is relaxed.
6. I give myself permission to rest and relax.
7. I am surrounded by peace and tranquility.
8. I handle stress with ease.
9. I am letting go of all my worries and fears.
10. Every breath I take fills me with calmness.
11. I am at peace with what is, what was, and what will be.
12. I deserve a break from my responsibilities.
13. I am relaxed, centered, and focused.
14. My body is relaxed, and my mind is calm.
15. I trust in the process of life.

16. I find joy in the simple moments.

17. I am grateful for this moment of peace.

18. I am letting go of all my stress.

19. I am in a state of peacefulness.

20. I am at peace with myself and the world around me.

21. I am worthy of a peaceful and stress-free life.

22. I am in harmony with my surroundings.

23. I choose to be calm and at peace.

24. I am capable of handling anything that comes my way.

25. I am free from stress and anxiety.

26. I am relaxed and at ease.

27. I am in a state of total relaxation.

28. I am letting go of all worries and embracing peace.

29. I am calm, composed, and confident.

30. I am a source of calmness for others.

31. I am in control of my thoughts and emotions.

32. I am at peace with my past, present, and future.

33. I embrace relaxation and let go of stress.

34. I am filled with a sense of tranquility.

35. I am free from the stress of others.

36. I am capable of finding peace in any situation.

37. I am at ease with myself and my surroundings.

38. I am grateful for moments of peace and relaxation.

39. I am in control of my stress and emotions.

40. I relax and let go of all tension.

41. I am a magnet for calmness and peace.

42. I am calm and serene in all situations.

43. I am thankful for moments of relaxation.

44. I am free from tension and anxiety.

45. I am in a state of deep relaxation.

46. I am at peace with the world around me.

47. I am relaxed and stress-free.

48. I am surrounded by calming energy.

49. I am capable of managing my stress.

50. I am calm, centered, and grounded.

51. I am a beacon of peace and calmness.

52. I am letting go of all stress and embracing peace.

53. I am at peace with my thoughts and feelings.

54. I am free from worry and stress.

55. I am in a state of complete relaxation.

56. I am calm, peaceful, and relaxed.

57. I am capable of finding calmness in any situation.

58. I am in harmony with my mind, body, and soul.

59. I am letting go of all tension and stress.

60. I am a vessel of peace and tranquility.

61. I am calm and at peace in all situations.

62. I am grateful for moments of peace and relaxation.

63. I am free from the stress of others.

64. I am capable of finding peace in any situation.

65. I am relaxed and stress-free.

66. I am in a state of deep relaxation.

67. I am at peace with the world around me.

68. I am surrounded by peace and tranquility.

69. I am in control of my stress levels.

70. I am grateful for moments of relaxation.

71. I am free from tension and anxiety.

72. I am letting go of all stress and embracing peace.

73. I am calm, composed, and confident.

74. I am in a state of total relaxation.

75. I am at peace with myself and the world around me.

76. I am deserving of peace and relaxation.

77. I am in harmony with my surroundings.

78. I am calm and serene in all situations.

79. I am a source of calmness for others.

80. I am letting go of all worries and embracing peace.

81. I am in control of my thoughts and emotions.

82. I am at peace with my past, present, and future.

83. I am free from stress and anxiety.

84. I am relaxed and at ease.

85. I am capable of handling anything that comes my way.

86. I am a magnet for calmness and peace.

87. I am in a state of peacefulness.

88. I am relaxed, centered, and focused.

89. I am grateful for this moment of peace.

90. I am in control of my stress and emotions.

91. I am relaxed and stress-free.

92. I am a vessel of peace and tranquility.

93. I am at peace with my thoughts and feelings.

94. I am capable of finding calmness in any situation.

95. I am free from worry and stress.

96. I am in a state of complete relaxation.

97. I am calm and at peace in all situations.

98. I am free from the stress of others.

99. I am capable of managing my stress.

100.   I am a beacon of peace and calmness.

CHAPTER 7: SELF-LOVE AND BODY POSITIVITY

1. I am worthy of love and respect.
2. My body is beautiful just the way it is.
3. I embrace my unique beauty.
4. I am enough, exactly as I am.
5. I love and accept myself unconditionally.
6. My body deserves love and care.
7. I am grateful for all that my body does for me.
8. I choose to nourish my body with healthy food and positive thoughts.
9. I celebrate my body and all its curves.
10. I am confident and radiant.
11. My worth is not defined by my appearance.
12. I am proud of what my body can achieve.
13. I release negative thoughts about my body.
14. I honor my body and treat it with kindness.

15. I am more than my body.

16. My self-worth is inherent and unchanging.

17. I am beautiful inside and out.

18. I am capable and strong.

19. I forgive myself and release the past.

20. I have the power to change my thoughts about my body.

21. I am deserving of all good things.

22. I trust my body and its wisdom.

23. I am grateful for my health and vitality.

24. My body is a vessel for my radiant spirit.

25. I am at peace with my body.

26. I choose to speak kindly to myself.

27. Every part of me is worthy of love.

28. I am a unique and valuable person.

29. I appreciate the beauty in my imperfections.

30. My body is my home, and I cherish it.

31. I am deserving of love, happiness, and respect.

32. I am proud of who I am becoming.

33. I celebrate my individuality.

34. I choose to see the good in myself.

35. I am a work of art, always evolving.

36. I am deserving of self-care and compassion.

37. I am resilient and brave.

38. I am beautiful in my own way.

39. I am grateful for my body's strength.

40. I am worthy of all the love I receive.

41. I am gentle with myself and my body.

42. I am a divine creation.

43. I treat my body with love and care.

44. I am proud of my journey and progress.

45. I am deserving of kindness and love.

46. I am enough, just as I am.

47. I love my body and all it does for me.

48. I am confident in my own skin.

49. I am grateful for my body's capabilities.

50. I am worthy of great things.

51. I honor the space I take up.

52. I am a masterpiece.

53. I embrace my body with love.

54. I am proud of my body's resilience.

55. I am beautiful, inside and out.
56. I am deserving of love and joy.
57. I am grateful for my unique body.
58. I am at peace with who I am.
59. I am deserving of all the good that life has to offer.
60. I am strong, capable, and worthy.
61. I am a beautiful person, inside and out.
62. I trust and respect my body.
63. I am proud of who I am.
64. I am deserving of love and respect, always.
65. I love myself completely and deeply.
66. I honor my body and treat it with kindness.
67. I am beautiful just the way I am.
68. I am grateful for my body's strength and resilience.
69. I am worthy of all the love and happiness in the world.
70. I am proud of my body and all it can do.
71. I am a unique and valuable person.
72. I am deserving of self-love and self-care.

73. I am confident and strong.

74. I am grateful for my health and well-being.

75. I am beautiful, powerful, and capable.

76. I forgive myself and embrace my imperfections.

77. I am deserving of all the good things in life.

78. I am proud of who I am and who I am becoming.

79. I am enough, just as I am.

80. I am worthy of love and respect, always.

81. I am confident in my own skin.

82. I am grateful for my body's capabilities.

83. I am deserving of love, happiness, and respect.

84. I am a masterpiece, always evolving.

85. I am beautiful, inside and out.

86. I am worthy of all the love I receive.

87. I am proud of my body's resilience.

88. I am deserving of kindness and love.

89. I am enough, just as I am.

90. I trust and respect my body.

91. I am gentle with myself and my body.

92. I am a divine creation.

93. I am proud of my journey and progress.

94. I honor the space I take up.

95. I treat my body with love and care.

96. I am grateful for my unique body.

97. I am at peace with who I am.

98. I am deserving of all the good that life has to offer.

99. I am strong, capable, and worthy.

100. I am a beautiful person, inside and out.

CHAPTER 8: ENERGY AND VITALITY

1. I am filled with energy and enthusiasm.
2. Vitality flows through my body effortlessly.
3. I embrace life with excitement and energy.
4. My body is a source of boundless energy.
5. Each day, I wake up feeling rejuvenated and energized.
6. My energy levels increase with each breath I take.
7. I am vibrant, energetic, and full of life.
8. Positive energy surrounds and fills me.
9. My mind and body are in perfect harmony, full of vitality.
10. I radiate energy and vitality.
11. I am naturally energetic and enthusiastic.
12. My spirit is vibrant and alive.
13. I have unlimited energy and stamina.
14. My body is strong and full of energy.
15. I attract positive energy with ease.
16. I am a powerhouse of energy and vitality.

17. My energy levels are constantly rising.
18. I am enthusiastic about life's opportunities.
19. I have an abundance of energy to accomplish my goals.
20. I am full of life and vitality.
21. I am grateful for the endless energy within me.
22. My cells are bursting with energy.
23. I am a magnet for positive energy.
24. I approach each day with vigor and passion.
25. I am an energetic person.
26. My body and mind are always in sync and full of energy.
27. I am alive, awake, and full of positive energy.
28. I am enthusiastic and passionate about everything I do.
29. My energy is boundless and flows freely.
30. I am constantly recharged with positive energy.

31. I greet each moment with enthusiasm and energy.

32. My body is a perfect vessel of vibrant energy.

33. I am energized by the love and joy in my life.

34. I am a beacon of positive energy and vitality.

35. My energy inspires others.

36. I am always full of vitality and enthusiasm.

37. I wake up each day feeling energized and ready.

38. I am excited about life and filled with energy.

39. My energy levels are always at their peak.

40. I am a dynamic and energetic person.

41. I am full of life force and vitality.

42. I have the energy to achieve all my dreams.

43. My enthusiasm for life is contagious.

44. I am full of zest and vitality.

45. I radiate vibrant energy wherever I go.

46. My body is energized and my mind is focused.
47. I fuel my body with healthy, energizing foods.
48. I am constantly overflowing with energy.
49. I am filled with vibrant energy every single day.
50. My soul is alive with energy and enthusiasm.
51. I am naturally energetic and full of life.
52. I am thankful for my vibrant health and energy.
53. I am a vibrant and dynamic person.
54. I am a source of positive energy.
55. Every cell in my body is alive with energy.
56. I am an enthusiastic and energetic individual.
57. My energy is limitless and never-ending.
58. I am a vessel of boundless energy.
59. I am alive with the energy of life.
60. I am constantly filled with vibrant energy.
61. I am enthusiastic and full of energy.

62. I am a bundle of positive energy.

63. My life is full of vitality and energy.

64. I am grateful for the energy that flows within me.

65. I am always energized and full of life.

66. My energy is vibrant and powerful.

67. I am a source of endless energy and vitality.

68. I am filled with dynamic energy and enthusiasm.

69. My body is a powerhouse of energy.

70. I am full of positive energy and vitality.

71. I am constantly recharged with life force.

72. I am a vibrant and energetic person.

73. I am enthusiastic and passionate about my life.

74. My energy is infectious and uplifting.

75. I am a beacon of vitality and enthusiasm.

76. I am filled with boundless energy.

77. My body and mind are always energized.

78. I am full of life and positive energy.

79. I am a dynamic and enthusiastic person.

80. My energy levels are always high.

81. I am always full of vibrant energy.

82. I am alive with enthusiasm and vitality.

83. My energy is limitless and abundant.

84. I am always enthusiastic and energetic.

85. I am a source of endless vitality.

86. I am filled with zest and enthusiasm for life.

87. I am constantly recharged with positive energy.

88. I am a vibrant and dynamic individual.

89. My energy is always at its peak.

90. I am full of life and positive energy.

91. I am enthusiastic about every aspect of my life.

92. My body is a wellspring of energy.

93. I am a magnet for positive, vibrant energy.

94. I am always energized and enthusiastic.

95. My spirit is alive with energy and enthusiasm.

96. I am a powerhouse of vitality and energy.

97. I am constantly filled with vibrant life force.

98. I am always full of energy and zest.

99. I am enthusiastic and full of life.

100.   I am grateful for the boundless energy within me.

CHAPTER 9: HOLISTIC HEALTH AND WELL-BEING

1. I am in perfect harmony with my mind, body, and spirit.
2. My body is healthy, my mind is calm, and my spirit is at peace.
3. I am grateful for the vibrant health that flows through me.
4. I nourish my body with healthy, whole foods.
5. I choose thoughts that support my overall well-being.
6. Every cell in my body is alive and full of energy.
7. I am connected to the healing power of the universe.
8. I am worthy of love, health, and happiness.
9. I am a radiant being filled with light and love.
10. My mind is clear and focused.

11. I listen to my body and give it what it needs.
12. My spirit is strong and resilient.
13. I am at peace with myself and the world around me.
14. I breathe deeply and fully, filling my body with life force.
15. I trust in the natural healing of my body.
16. I am surrounded by positive and loving energy.
17. I am aligned with the highest frequency of love and well-being.
18. My body is a temple of vibrant health.
19. I honor my body by taking time to rest and rejuvenate.
20. I release any tension and stress from my body and mind.
21. I am grateful for the gift of another healthy day.
22. I am open to receiving healing energy from the universe.
23. I am grounded, centered, and at peace.

24. My mind, body, and spirit are in perfect balance.
25. I am a magnet for health, wealth, and happiness.
26. I am in tune with the rhythm of life.
27. I radiate positive energy and attract positive experiences.
28. I am a beacon of love and light.
29. I trust my intuition and follow its guidance.
30. I am connected to the infinite wisdom of the universe.
31. I am open to the abundance of health and well-being in my life.
32. I am grateful for the love and support that surrounds me.
33. I embrace the present moment with an open heart.
34. My heart is open to giving and receiving love.
35. I am a beautiful being of light and love.

36. I am in control of my thoughts and emotions.
37. I choose to see the good in every situation.
38. I am a powerful creator of my reality.
39. I am surrounded by loving and supportive people.
40. I am worthy of a healthy and fulfilling life.
41. I trust in the process of life.
42. I am a vessel of peace and tranquility.
43. I am grateful for my strong, healthy body.
44. I am at one with the universe.
45. I am constantly growing and evolving.
46. I am a reflection of divine love and light.
47. I am at peace with my past, present, and future.
48. I am free from worry and fear.
49. I am a positive thinker and only attract positivity into my life.
50. I am strong, capable, and resilient.
51. I am deserving of all the good things life has to offer.
52. I am in perfect health.

53. I am surrounded by healing energy.
54. I am grateful for the abundance of health in my life.
55. I am always learning and growing.
56. I am at peace with myself and others.
57. I am a loving and compassionate being.
58. I am grateful for the love and support in my life.
59. I am in alignment with my highest self.
60. I am a beacon of love and hope.
61. I am open to new and exciting possibilities.
62. I am a vessel of peace and calm.
63. I am grateful for my healthy mind and body.
64. I am surrounded by positive energy.
65. I am a powerful creator of my own reality.
66. I am worthy of love and respect.
67. I am at peace with who I am.
68. I am a reflection of divine light and love.
69. I am open to the healing power of nature.
70. I am grateful for the abundance in my life.

71. I am a loving and kind person.
72. I am connected to the infinite wisdom of the universe.
73. I am a positive thinker and attract positivity into my life.
74. I am at peace with my journey.
75. I am a beacon of light and love.
76. I am worthy of a healthy and happy life.
77. I am in perfect harmony with myself and the world around me.
78. I am a reflection of divine love and light.
79. I am open to the healing power of the universe.
80. I am grateful for the love and support in my life.
81. I am a loving and compassionate being.
82. I am in alignment with my highest self.
83. I am a vessel of peace and calm.
84. I am a powerful creator of my own reality.
85. I am deserving of all the good things life has to offer.
86. I am in perfect health.

87. I am surrounded by healing energy.
88. I am grateful for the abundance of health in my life.
89. I am always learning and growing.
90. I am at peace with myself and others.
91. I am a loving and kind person.
92. I am a reflection of divine light and love.
93. I am open to the healing power of nature.
94. I am grateful for the abundance in my life.
95. I am a positive thinker and attract positivity into my life.
96. I am at peace with my journey.
97. I am a beacon of light and love.
98. I am worthy of love and respect.
99. I am in perfect harmony with myself and the world around me.
100. I am a reflection of divine love and light.

BOOKS BY AUTHOR

Scan here to read.

9 Secrets of Subconscious Mind for Manifesting the Desired Outcomes

Scan here to read.

Rewire Your Beliefs: Eliminate Limiting Beliefs, Stop Negative Thinking, Use Empowering Affirmations, and Transform Your Mind.

Scan here to read

Secrets of Happy Life - Conquer Your Inner World with Positive Self-talk. Master the Art of Forgiveness and Experience Joy. Fill Your Heart with Love and compassion.

Scan here to read

Everyday Happiness: 21 Tiny Habits to Conquer Your Stress, Experience Joy and Have a Content Life.

Scan here to read

7 Timeless Principles to Cultivate Love, Deepen Understanding, and Perpetuate Mutual Respect Among Loved Ones.

Scan here to read

66 Quick Prompts to Transcend Sadness, Embrace Happiness, Unveiling the Secrets to Lasting Joy.

Scan here to read

100 Powerful Thoughts to Empower Self-Confidence, Cultivate Resilience, and Illuminate the Path to Joyful

Scan here to read

Positive Affirmations For Success: Create Goal Clarity, Cultivate Discipline for Focus, and Boost Confidence to Achieve Success.

Scan here to read

Unlock Your Subconscious Mind: 5 Steps Formula to Conquer Negative Beliefs, Foster Positive Change, and Manifest the Desired Outcome Faster.

Scan here to read

Conquer Financial Challenges, Master Wealth Creation, And Achieve Lasting Financial Freedom.

ABOUT AUTHOR

Dipaali Ghanshyam Patel is a dedicated life coach, inner wellness advocate, and author passionate about transforming lives through mental health and happiness. Having overcome her own struggles with low self-esteem, negative thinking, and limiting beliefs, Dipaali discovered the power of continuous learning, meditation, and affirmations in reshaping her subconscious mind.

Her personal journey from feeling unloved and unsupported to achieving profound personal breakthroughs inspires her mission to help others unlock their potential. Through her books, workshops, and online courses, Dipaali offers practical tools and techniques to identify and eliminate subconscious limiting beliefs, empowering readers to create positive, fulfilling lives.

With a commitment to promoting mental well-being, Dipaali teaches the art of meditation and the science of affirmations, guiding individuals to train their subconscious minds for lasting success and happiness.

Visit her website www.dipaali.life and Join Dipaali on a transformative journey to harness the power of your mind, overcome challenges, and design a life filled with joy and prosperity. Let her experiences and insights be your roadmap to a brighter, more empowered future.

BIG ASK

Visit my website and join my community for a transformative workshop that is ongoing and upcoming, where we will together spread INNER Purity into the outer world.

I kindly ask you to rate and write a review as an act of kindness. Your review holds importance to me and will positively impact humanity.

Rate and review my google profile

Google/Dipaali-life